Nova Scotia:

Nova Scotia: **Window on the Sea**

Nova Scotia:
Window on the Sea

Text by Ernest Buckler
Photographs by Hans Weber

McClelland and Stewart Limited

©Ernest Buckler and Hans Weber
1973
Reprinted 1974
0-7710-4690-1

The Canadian Publishers
McClelland and Stewart Limited
Illustrated Book Division
25 Hollinger Road, Toronto

Design: David Shaw

Printed and bound in Canada

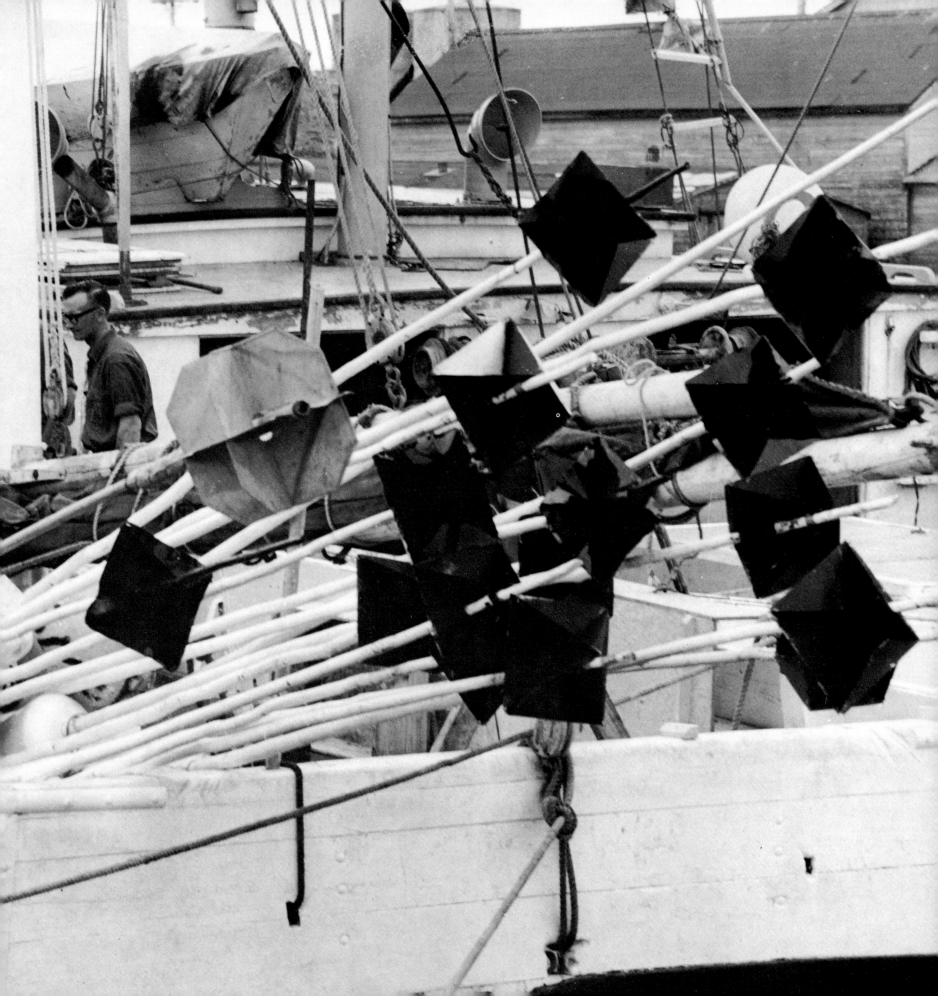

Contents

Amethysts and Dragonflies

Nova Scotia is nearly an island, nearly the last place left where place and people are not thinned and adulterated with graftings that grow across the grain. Yet what saves it from insularity is a peninsularity like that of the heart. The arteries go out to the Main, but the beat is all of itself.

Sometimes it seems self-contradictory. It is grounded in the sea, but rooted in the land. Its features are as varied as those of the body.

As the hand is entirely different from the eye, so is the ripple of breeze, weighted with light, that shot-silks the strawberried grass in the peace-rivered Gaspereau different from the hippopotamus rocks the elemental sea fumes against in a thunderstorm at Peggy's Cove.

As the throat is entirely different from the lung, so is the everlasting shudder of Time in Port Royal (where North America started) different from the Now-light in the eyes of children swimming in the meadow brook when the last load of hay they've raked after has been landed in the sweltering barn.

Yet as the body is "one", for all its variousness, so is Nova Scotia. Its capes, coves, lochs, bays and harbours jigsaw its coastline as if whoever was its architect had let his pencil stray without direction. Yet it remains a whole.

Its mountains take on no Cabot lordliness. They chat like uncles with their nephew valleys. Even the rocks have no stoniness. Houses (though their eyes may be as different as brothers' from cousins' or great-aunts') agree with each other, noddingly, and swap kinship the day long.

In its cities or near-cities (other than Halifax, where the myth-softened mask of a history which has been unique as nowhere else pervades even the impervious) pavements, as in cities everywhere, beat the faces blind. But elsewhere people keep their hearts on the latch.

Men at Grand Pré, tired to blurring, knock clods of earth off the ploughshare that has turned the last restorative furrow in the clover field and, long after Evangeline, west their feet homeward to suppertime and what is still the spirit of lantern light.

Men, blurred by faith (though not scared of the sacred) light candles in the great cathedral at Church Point which overawes the patient waterside like Christ Galilee.

Men at Sober Island sink nets into the sombre sea and draw up its deep (the mackerel gasping like thought with its mouth open) hand over rope-storied hand.

Men at Beaver River shock the living slumber out of giant maples with their gleaming axe blades before they fell them in a sweep majestic as the fall of empires, their muscles sterner than bone in the frozen day.

Men in Cape Breton go down into the dark of the earth for the wood of eons made coal....

But they are all the same kind of man.

Sober Island. Wine Harbour. Folly Lake. Bible Brook.... Some of the place names sound quaint. But the people are not.

They are no quainter than trees. Their faces may be gnarled as knuckles. They may be wrenched from any formal beauty by the erosion of dailiness. But they are not shuttered by the city wariness, not scoundreled by the lie of openness assumed, not mineralized by the poison pellet at the core of all tyrannical ambition. Their eyes see through sham at a glance; but they are not themselves contagioned by it or squinted or gimleted.

Some people are dilettantes of themselves. Nova Scotians people ply their own verb for all it's worth. Each is himself because he does not imitate — any more than a tree tries to turn itself into a geranium.

In the great cities, man is forever lonely because he never sees his thoughts and feelings corporified outside him, so that the crush of their edgelessness is lessened. In Nova Scotia, no man but can see (whether he sees what he sees or not) the shape of his thoughts and feelings in print, so to speak, almost everywhere he looks or hears:

The elixir of winning in the sound of the pine trees making their own breeze.

The gusts of longing for someone gone that bend the heart so low no sigh can do anything to exhale them, in the stretching fields that shimmer the greener for the very nowhereness in them of the one who was once your everywhere.

The gull-shaped thought in the thought-shaped gull.

The sheen of health in the bluejay's wing.

The pang of age first seen as the one thing that never stops for a moment's recess, in the calendered beech leaves.

The bound of joy, in the sound of the sun-up nails being driven into the concurring boards in the house the man is building for his family in sight of the tidal river.

The dinginess (yes, that too) of those days when the windows in the lighthouse of the mind are streaked with the grime of failed hopes, when you feel you are neglectable in the eyes of others (as in your own you are no more than a neglectable question), when everything is now diminished to itself divided by a thousand — there it is in the scrawny featherless necks of the four fledgling sparrows huddled dead in the rain-soaked nest.

The tawdriness of the mind's sullen moment picking its teeth — there it is in the Javex can made into a windmill at the end of the unweeded driveway where it meets the asphalt....

But never farther off than the unspoken can reach is the surety that gives a man his cadence: in the stormproof forests and the everlasting sea.

Nowhere flawlessly beautiful, Nova Scotia is often for that very reason the more beautiful, as one face is sometimes lovelier to another for its very plainnesses.

Neither stately nor mansioned in any one quality, it has yet a watermark all its own which it stamps (invisibly but no less distinguishably) on each of its particulars. Though they are as multiform as the bibliography of seed.

It is amethysts in the imperial rocks at Blomidon, and snow apples in the consentful orchards of the Valley.

It is a black bear in the blueberry barrens, and the sun afternooning on the village grave of a child aged six.

It is the train blowing lonesome as Lincoln's at all the crossings from Yarmouth to Hawkesbury, and the leap of the confettied trout in the stream that feeds the sawmill where the fresh-cut shingles smell clean as morning.

It is the grey December blizzard, hard-hearted as sleeplessness, that unites everything it scourges, from the careworn house on the speechless hill to the house proud of the street it's on . . . and the April breeze, its penitence, that awakens the seed to its future.

It is the oxen of the muscle and the cavalry (or the Calvary) of the senses.

It is picks and shovels and canoes (which, another way, spell "oceans") and shotguns (which, another way, misspell "snug").

It is the terrible silences in the breast of the man whose wage permits his family little more than bread, and the thunderclap of rum and harmonicas.

It is silver birches (and their shadows) in the silver moonlight.

It is the sun coming up like an anthem behind the daily hills, and the sun descending into the haunts of yesterday where those moments charged with the light and conclusions of life are so deathlessly kept . . . .

Here, each man has seen the pear blossom, all perfection, and smelled the wild roses on the stone wall.

He has felt the heart's rejoicing and the heart's face fall.

He has held, long and hard, those things that the arms or the eyes can hold (the flesh, the present images), and he has gazed, heart-staggered, at the flesh not there, at the touch refused. At the information of what the arms or the eyes can never quite reach:

The dragonfly rising from the landlocked brook, its wings a shimmer as they hold it absolutely still, to make its statement on the boundless air.

The wild geese flying arrowed, their statement with them, into the indecipherable clouds.

The hush of meaning that the train whistle dying out has made form of....

He has seen the *natural*, with its grace never learned, but never insecure like learning's:

The sap (by its own command) rising in the sugar maple.

The apple (by its own map) shaping itself on the bough.

The daisy forming its own petals as no human conjurer could.

The earth itself living out what it was born with, totally without artifice....

Nova Scotia is the face from Genesis and the face from Ruth. The face from Greco and the face from Rubens. The life from Faulkner and the life from Hardy....

It is a dictionary where the seasons look up their own meanings and test them. It is a sea-son where men can man their own helms.

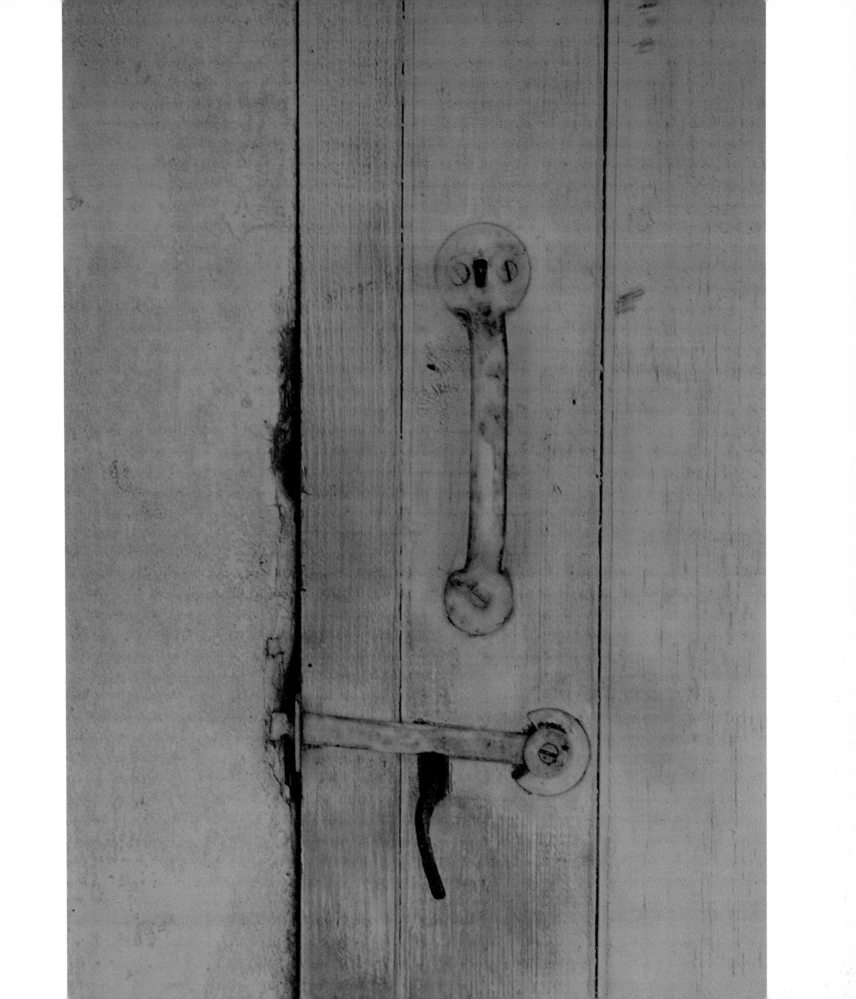

Man and Snowman

If the sea infixes some nameless and unslakeable yearning in a man's eyes, the farm yokes the facts of memory to his every breath. And more than the fisherman with his single-hearted gaze, he comes to be the sum, substance and museum of its thronging assembly.

A farmer, age upon him, lies on his bed at Bras d'Or. (Or it could be Christmas Island or Sheet Harbour.) His body, twin of him, has betrayed him.

The strange thing, there had never been any pain. Not even at the start. Just that painless blow somewhere inside his head as he lifted the wig of hay from the rack, so heavy the fork buckled with it. It was like a hammer blow of sound, and then his left side going dead like a sound gone.

He couldn't remember being carried from the barn. But when he came to in his bedroom his mind was as clear as it had ever been. He could see. He could hear. But he couldn't move his head, or walk alone — or speak.

They put a slate beside his good hand. (An old one of his own he thought it must be, for children had not used slates these many years.) On it he could write down any questions he had, or tell them of any needs.

He hadn't written a word since he left school: at fourteen, because his own aging father had needed his stout muscle on the farm. The slate pencil, his most likely too, felt clumsy in his fingers. But he could make himself understood.

The family (his son and his son's wife and the grandchildren, Mark and Paul) felt none of that burdensome recoil so often touched off by sickness in the old. They tended him as involvedly as if he was nineteen.

At first they'd come into his bedroom every evening and tell him all that had happened that day. What they'd done. The people they'd seen. What they'd heard and what they thought about it. Down to the last detail.

But gradually, a proud man, he came to discourage this demand on them.

Gradually, not to bother them, he ceased to write any questions on the slate. Now, all he wrote was "yes" or "no".

"Are you all right?"

"Yes."

"Do you want anything?"

"No."

Sometimes he wanted death. Anything to free him from the silence the walls ticked with and the pattern of purple ivy that stamped itself so tirelessly on the wallpaper. But he never wrote anything like that.

They never neglected him. They never left him alone in the house. And tied to his spool bed, on the rung nearest his good hand, was a bell he could ring if he had to get out onto the "chair". A tinkler off the string of sleighbells he had himself sewn to the leather thongs the day he drove Ellen in to town to marry her.

He minded the chair as nothing in his life before. Even when the son came. When the wife came it was agony. And once while she was bathing him and at the pressure of the warm cloth he came alive down there he had never felt so bitterly reduced.

They switched his bed around so that his head faced the window. So that he could see nearly all the fields and the movements in them, and the pasture that ran back to the steep spruce mountain.

He watched them sow the seeds in the land he'd been the first to break. He watched them hay where he had sown the first clover. The silence ceased to tick then.

But he couldn't see the path that led to the meadow. He couldn't see the grove of saplings where the son used to play under his eye while he cut the hoop poles. And sometimes, when a movement would vanish beyond the edges of the rectangle of fields the window framed, he would feel like tearing the walls apart.

But his back was in no way broken. He was the man who can bear more than he can bear.

"I think he might," she said. "Yesterday when I took the broth up to him I told him I'd made it from the two partridge you'd shot for him in that wild apple tree at the edge of the burntland. I think he understood."

"And do you remember way back at the first?" he said. "When he kept writing 'deed' on the slate and we thought it was 'dead' and he was wandering? Until Paul —wasn't it?—guessed that what he wanted was to make the place over to me while he could still sign?"

"Yes." She smiled. "It's funny about the children," she said. "Most children shy away from anyone sick. But Paul and Mark . . . if they've made something in school . . . or anything . . . the first thing they get into the house they run up to show him. Before they even take their coats off. I never have to ask them to."

"Kids always liked him," the son said. "And it was strange, because he never made that much fuss over them. He was always just so . . . well, steady. He never let bad luck—or bad news—or anything else—get the best of him." His eyes went suddenly still. "I only ever seen him cry but the once. It was one day he didn't have the money to take me to the circus in town." His eyes came back as breath does after a sigh. "Do you think I should tell him about Leo, then?"

"I would."

"All right," the son said. "I'll tell him in the morning."

. . . 25 . . . .

That was the city block.

For a moment a greyness the shade of the brain's own grey shadowed his mind as it does when you recall some step in your life so mistaken that it seems to have been the act of a total stranger. Another moment and the dimness vanished in the light of the memory's sheer chiseling force.

At first the thought of working in the city, if only at a flagman's job with a con- struction crew, was all excitement. The wheels of the train taking him there had

seemed like a steed of adventure he was riding. It overrode even the imprint of
Ellen's face (fixed in its last look as the faces of people you leave are, and stationary
as italics) at the station.

But after a week of nights in the rented room, a sense of suffocation grew.

The room's walls seemed to wall in all the scuffed fallout of the shabby dreams
(or had there been any at all?) of the men (their lives rented, too, as cheaply as pos-
sible) who had stared at this ceiling before him. He began to feel as if the tale of his
own life was not in ink of any kind but in chalk.

The months went by like blinded oxen. This feeling of emptiness went deeper
and deeper.

Here, in the city, it was as if, though nothing ever stood still, nothing moved. He
had never taken orders (except from the sun). Here, he had to take orders, without
question, from a man whose back he could have broken with one hammerlock of
his plough-hardened muscles.

And every day the innumerable blows on his huddled homesick heart. From
the scabrous state that city things (like drunks) fall into. Or from the oblivious:

Scum-sloshed pilings in the bilgewater of the harbour.

Tram cars, bound to their tracks, climbing the hilly streets, with all their
occupants so glazed with monotony that none of them notices how streets can
choke the life-reach out of hills even.

Sirens screaming fire; and other (silent) sirens screaming accidents to the spirit,
itself too dulled to know the grazing wound from the fatal.

Water besmirching itself in the gutter where the sodden poster lies.

Clouds beclouding themselves with puzzlement at the scrambled alphabet
below.

Labels, labels, labels, everywhere . . . loudmouthing the trivial contents they
enwrap.

No singing birds.

No gladness in the fountain in the Mall.

No two things, however close, less than the distance of effigies apart. Neither the bottle caps and the slush beneath the rusted sign with the capitals missing. Nor the amusements like the gargoyles of fun, and the endless Sundays when the blind factory windows (and the prison eyes in the locked-up shops) out-hollow the hollow church bells until it becomes as when not even the letters of your own name stir any response in you.

The trees in the park so captive and denatured that they impose a gloss of loneliness even lonesomer than the sleepwalking movements of the men and women indoored at the same worthless tasks day in and day out.

The crumpled bill that is the only link between the merchant and his customer.

The telephone poles that bear the wires overhead, that are as deaf as money to the messages they bear; as deaf as the object longing seeks to the cries within the messages that swarm through them....

And in the street:

The boss-faced men, and the clock-stopped faces of the others.

The faces that look like an article of clothing bought uncertainly and never worn thereafter with satisfaction.

The faces that look as if they had been slept (or nightmared) in.

Men's hands womanized by pen and paper.

The eyes that neither give nor lend nor borrow.

The mouths like a "fault" in cement, looking as if they were clamped tight on their own curb bits....

Sometimes the city like some monstrous dragon in a child's dream of dragons he'd seen on a page, the soot of exile fuming from its nostrils. Sometimes like a giant shell-backed insect on its back, its million legs flailing helplessly in the air....

Until one day near the end of this first crippling year there he caught a glimpse in the street of a girl's face so like Ellen's, so (with all the grit that plunders the flesh left out) like a vision of Ellen's, that he was staggered.

That afternoon when the foreman shouted at him, "Get a move on there! What the hell do you think you're doin', havin' your picture taken?", he gave him his fist in the greatest hallelujah it had ever felt.

That night he took the midnight train home.

. . . 25, 30, 35, 40, 45, 50. . . .
A single pattern made these blocks as one.

It was eating with Ellen, sleeping with Ellen, working with Ellen, laughing with Ellen, having Ellen to turn to. . . .

It was being each other's total hearer and hearth.

It was having every threat a safety away from striking him on any naked nerve, because loving Ellen was the nerve of him that cushioned all the rest from the last thing that nerves can not withstand: forlornness.

(It was a little like being freedomly stormstayed inside a warm cordial house that has the spirit of mulled wine.)

Smoke rising, dew falling, wheels turning, sun, rain, snow . . . with Ellen there, it was having all the good things in the year's teeming calendar as near to him as the touch of his own blood and all the stony ones a flint-proof skin apart.

It was day after day of wholeness without a sliver of hankering to enpustule it.

It was putting his own son on the horse's back when he ploughed.

It was the daily bread of hope not bred in doubt — but more than hope, it was home.

Ellen . . . Ellen . . . Ellen. . . . Her name flaked down through his mind as gently as the snowflakes eddied down outside the window, and he slept. He slept, and he dreamed.

He dreamed about the night Ellen died, the year he was 50.

He saw the burning sunset paint the colours of pain he'd never felt the likes of, on the blind church windows. He felt the beating his heart took from the skulls of everything he looked at that her hands would never touch again or her eyes ever see. Each leaf, each stone, each blade of grass, had printed on it, each in its own alphabet, the one word "gone"—each of them itself as if gone out of reach. He saw the gaping socket of unrelatedness inside him, now that she was forever out of sight....

He awoke, nearly choked with the sound of crying his throat couldn't make.

Downstairs, the wife was hearing young Paul's spellings.

"Trance . . . Tranquil . . . Transient . . . ."

"What does 'transient' mean?" Paul asked.

She didn't know. She looked at her husband.

"I don't know, either," he said. "Go find it in that big dictionary of your grandfather's." He looked at the sunset that was all bruise and flame. "You know," he said slowly, "he hardly went to school much, but he was always reading. Anything he could get hold of. He knew what all kinds of long words meant. If he'd been born somewhere else . . . ."

"I'm not so sure," the wife said. "You could never get him to talk about that time he spent in the city, could you."

"He slept a lot today," she added. "I think he's failing."

"Maybe . . . a little," the son said. "But he always had that strong constitution."

"What does 'constitution' mean?" Paul asked.

The dream slipped away to wherever dreams go, taking its freight of feeling with it. His mind went back to his game. Or was it a task now? There was a new sense of urgency about it. A sudden drive to have it over with.

. . . 55, 60, 65 . . . .

Yes, yes, those blocks too were fairly clear. Clear enough, anyway, that in this new haste to reach the end he could skip them, come back to them later. Fill them in later, once the capstone block of 70 was, all conquered, fitted into place.

For they were lasting, simply. Finding out that if you put the sickened heart to work again, and soon, a different set of scopes and muscles grew. Finding that whatever life might rob you of, you were always left with *something* worth its cost. Learning that . . . .

But surely all you had learned, any answers there might be, would be contained in that last block.

He skipped to 70.

"I left his window up a crack this afternoon," the wife said, "to air the room out. Paul, would you go up and put it down? It looks like rain. But don't disturb him."

. . . 70 . . . 70 . . . 70 . . . .

His mind wrestled with it. But in a kind of dismay he found he couldn't force it into the shape of anything whatsoever.

He was completely blocked. Why, why, he asked himself, could he call up those early years so easily and yet be helpless to picture the day he was 70? A day that was hardly a month ago, he was sure.

Again and again he tried. But each time, his mind caught itself, before he knew it, slewing backward. 60, 60, 60 . . . so many measures! 60 seconds in a minute . . . 60 minutes in an hour . . . 60 pounds in a bushel of potatoes . . . 60 degrees (and where was his carpenter's protractor now?) in each angle of a rafter wedge that had all sides the same . . . .

Again and again he reined his mind back to its object, trying to storm the image of his seventieth birthday clear. But again and again he met only a wall blanker than smoke, a nowhere louder than silence, a stare whiter than zeroes. Again . . . and again . . . and again . . . .

Until, quite suddenly, as when you step into the star-cooled clearing after a day with the axe in the knotted thicket of rock hemlock that you hadn't given up on until it was all felled and limbed and piled . . . as then, a wash of total serenity went through and through him.

He didn't touch the bell. But he reached for the slate pencil in the dark.

The rain started softly, as if it was picking its steps; then poured in earnest all night long.

The snow forts were dissolved, and the snowman melted gradually until there was nothing left of it but the coals and the pipe and the hat, drenched dark, but with the darker sweat stains on the band still showing.

In the morning, when the son went into the bedroom and found his father dead, there was one word scrawled on the slate. None of them could puzzle it out for certain.

The wife thought it was "please". The son, "praise". Mark thought it was "price".

"No, no," Paul said, "it's 'peace'."

"How old was he?" the woman who wrote up deaths for the town newspaper asked.

"Not quite seventy," the wife said. "Not till this coming Friday. The date's right there in the Bible."

"He always had a strong constitution, didn't he," Paul said, nearly crying but proud of this word he'd learned.

"Yes," the father said. "He had his good times and his bad times . . . but if anyone ever had the stuff in him . . . or got the most out of life . . . *he* did."

Faces and Universes

To speak of Nova Scotia is not to speak of its thoroughfares of traffic, business, learning.... These are the same here as everywhere: where the din of striving and the tin of words deface the face and put the price tags on it. The heart of this province is, rather, the province of the heart: in its enclaves of farm and seaside village.

But it is no Elysium, no cure-all.

Here, starker than anywhere else, are the reminders of how inexorably one's address shifts from the letter to the tombstone; of what useless armour is the scarecrow, Thought, against the crows of Time.

To the already downhearted it is a land melancholy beyond description. Go there so lonely that each breath is another burning sup, deeper than pain, not from the air but from the airlessness inside you . . . and (both painter and sculptor of sentience incarnate) it will show you a statement of loneliness so far outmatching yours (though turned unreachably away from any link with it) that your breath will be nearly stripped from flesh by echoes of the unutterable:

A field of snow, dead of infinity before it fell, outdistancing its own eye as it stretches toward the gun-metal band of frozen light that bars all entrances to the horizon.

Beauty burning in each autumned leaf with the bladed light of all that's irrecoverable.

Unknown children, out of hearing, throwing a ball against the rain-eaten shingles of an unknown barn.

The last tree on the ridge of a slope down to the wanderer river.

A beam of moonlight striking the gilded fringe on the marker in the church Bible, open to Deuteronomy, and unseen from Sunday to Sunday.

A wild aster, a weed thinking it's a flower, blooming alone in the abandoned marsh.

A row of stakes leaning against the February dusk.

A face now but a shell of all its Junes.

A track.

Counterfeit and Coin

The handwriting is on the well—and on the dory. The spirit of *this* Nova Scotia seems to be fast disappearing to wherever the spirit of a countryside flees when others than the planters put their brass and specious touch on it. Whether (opinions differ) an occasion for hurrah or alas—"progress," the advance spy of Babel and steel, has already begun to infiltrate and infest the land, begun to shoulder its individuality aside and mark it out for parcelment.

Already in some districts the box-eyed houses, some of them with box-eyed occupants, are trying to make conformity regnant; trying to tame by imprisonment in the dismal plots of their backyards the grass that was once (with the trees) king of the whole landscape. The land is beginning to smother beneath all the crockery of man that is being heaped on it.

Brick stares where wood used to smile. Bulldozers disrespect stones that men were once proud to lift. Shopping Centres (with their aisles of marked-down goods putting as if an ash on the quick of the crowd-drubbed faces of the people who wander them) spring up where once were orchards. Television aerials comb the night for dross or screams where once the night kissed righteous muscles with the balm of rest. Faces in the bus, travelling like luggage (while the air brakes unconsciously shunt their breath more dreadfully than a sigh of Christ's, and the skimmed-eyed waitresses at the midway restaurant brace the counter with stoups of caffeine and cruets of vinegar for the daily gut of loneliness), scan each other's locks where faces once were joined by glances as if by hyphens of light. Doubts lean where certainties once stood. . . .

And yet. And yet in other districts there are still things like these:

Kingfishers still circle the meadows. Pebbles pure-white as the first particle that knew it was silver jewel the beds of innocent brooks. Gods of primal force, like Thors and Odins to the man's own trifling strength, both awe and exhilarate him as they ride the chain lightning or walk on the shoulders of mountains beneath the frost-glint of stars. A man carries his son home on his shoulders after a long day's mission blazing lines in the holy forest. Neighbours enact their substantive noun when there's a neighbour's sickness in the night; as friends do theirs, the cindered and the green times through. Children laugh without being told what's funny. Un-citied weathers still find an untouched place to be themselves. Partridges, alert as trigonometry, still feed on the crimson seed sacs of the wild roses, and ferns the height of deer still ennoble the air around them like Plantagenets the field of honour. Some houses are still chroniclers, some hills still revelations—it is in these places that it can be seen how Nova Scotians own the sighting of their own eyes as few men do.

The born Nova Scotian owns his own name and answers to it without hesitation at the challenge of whatever roll call. He owns his own blood. And his is the most remembering of all bloods. The tincture of heritage from that of his forbears is always constitutively in him in the miraculous way that a single tear is said to tincture, with its disinfectant, seas of water; in the way that a man's resemblance to his great-grandparent across the forehead is transmitted in a pinpoint of sperm. Even now, the gait of original freedom stubbornly in him and his fellows, he never has to go far to find another Nova Scotian with a like spine: to match itself against annihilation by the juggernaut which levels all things to sameness. Enough of these men may yet stop it dead in its tracks. Their spirit may yet prevail, as the simplest green plant can split the clench of stone and break out its green leaves above it.

Faith (and where else can faith for the future be placed?) must look too to the young. Here as elsewhere they are often labelled slovenly, rootless, nothing but destructive . . . all that. But the best of them (who are by far the greater majority) have seen through the trinkets of material success, have (with their acute ear) heard the rattle of dry bones in the sepulchral vaults where "familiars" of the megamachine reside, and are not prepared to buy with their lives the fat and fictions of the plush-lined occupation. In growing numbers they are searching for work that